The Re-entry Roadmap

The Re-entry Roadmap

The Re-entry Roadmap

Find Your Best Next Step
After Living Abroad

Cate Brubaker, PhD

Thinking Travel Press

The Re-entry Roadmap
Copyright © 2020 by Cate Brubaker, Small Planet Studio, LLC

All rights reserved. No part of this publication may be reproduced, distributed, or transmitted in any form or by any means, including by photocopying, recording, or other electronic or mechanical methods, without the prior written permission of the publisher, except in the case of brief quotations embodied in critical reviews and certain other noncommercial uses permitted by copyright law.

Edition 3.5: July 2020

ISBN: 978-0692138182 (Thinking Travel Press)

Cover design by Dylan Mierzwinski & Cate Brubaker
Editing by Rachel Radway
Book design by Cate Brubaker

This workbook is intended for individual personal use.

If you'd like to share the Re-entry Roadmap with a fellow returnee, send them to:

https://smallplanetstudio.com/rr

***

Want to use this workbook with your students or coaching clients?

For more information about our special bulk discount rate,
please contact the author directly at:

https://smallplanetstudio.com/contact

***

Work with study abroad students?

Check out our Study Abroad Re-entry Toolkit here:

https://smallplanetstudio.com/study-abroad-reentry-toolkit

The Re-entry Roadmap

For Aaron, always.

"The world of international education is full of opportunity and challenge. Leaders and teachers considering new positions devote significant time and study as they compare positions and locations around the world. But few take the time to consider the implications of returning home. New experiences shape our perspectives whether we realize it or not. The Re-entry Roadmap thoughtfully guides expectations and readjustment."
—Jane Larsson, Executive Director, Council of International Schools

"There are two tests for any type of re-entry preparation, whether a workshop, a book, or a workbook: it should address the core challenges of reverse culture shock and at the same time convey the impression that these mountains really can be climbed. Cate's book passes the first test with great skill and imagination, and as for the second: there's every chance returnees will put this book down and think 'I *can* do this!' What more could we ask?"
—Craig Storti, author of *The Art of Coming Home* and *Why Travel Matters*

"The Re-entry Roadmap is a comprehensive guide to returning 'home' without parking your adventures. Packed with reflective tools, new perspectives and helpful hints, Cate's workbook will help you reframe your re-entry, and use it as an opportunity to identify what you really want going forwards. I wish I had had a copy when I went through re-entries.
A must-have companion for your re-entry!"
—Helen Watts, Re-entry coach at *WattsYourPathway*

"Without question, the Re-entry Roadmap is a must-have for anyone facing re-entry!"
—Jodi Harris, *World Tree Coaching*

"Students who (re)enter their home countries for university become an 'invisible immigrant,' they look the same but feel different and are often left to navigate their (re)entry alone. Dr. Brubaker's brilliantly practical workbook guides adult learners/global souls through the important reflections, observations, and conversations that are essential to supporting a successful re-entry."
—Hannah Morris & Megan Norton, *Intercultural Transitions*

"The Re-entry Roadmap is a thorough and well curated pathway to navigating the convoluted world of re-entry. Cate's combination of reflective questions and down-to-earth exercises is guaranteed to sooth re-entry woes and provide context to an alienating experience. Cate has provided the thinking tools that when applied can change the trajectory of your re-entry and your next adventure.
Read it, study it and do the work to reap the benefits."
—Doreen M. Cumberford, *International Transitions Coach*

"Everyone who goes abroad should have a copy of this book when coming back—actually, it should be sold in the duty free shop before going through customs. It is THAT good and essential."
—Pamela Viviana Arraras, *International Teacher*

"When it comes to cross-cultural re-entry/return, Cate Brubaker leads the pack! Far more than a simple workbook for dealing with the ups and downs of returning from a global adventure, The Re-Entry Roadmap is a guided tour by a seasoned escort who really knows how to navigate the re-entry terrain."
—Linda Janssen, author of *The Emotionally Resilient Expat: Engage, Adapt and Thrive Across Cultures*

"I love the reflection exercises and tips, which help guide you through processing those complex emotions and channel them toward something constructive."
—Michelle Chang, *Intentional Travelers*

"I love, love, love the mind map spaces available to write about yourself before, during, and after abroad. Anyone in 'abroad limbo' would benefit from the exercises and introspection activities, helping them to really get their global thoughts, feelings, and goals on paper and turning them into a tangible global life."
—Kerianne Baylor, *Think Global School*

"OH MY GOODNESS! This practical workbook is the FIRST book you should read…and perhaps the only one!"
—*Amazon Reviewer*

"LOVE this book. Very down to earth with a sense of humor."
—*Amazon Reviewer*

"This book is a great tool! If you are currently at loose ends after time abroad, grab this book! Cate Brubaker asks questions that will get you thinking, appreciating, and looking ahead. It's like sitting with a good friend and ranting, laughing, and brainstorming your way into a future that delights you. And at the end you'll have a visual reminder of who you are, what you've experienced, how you've grown, and where you're headed."
—*Amazon Reviewer*

"I returned from living in China for over nine years, and this was by far the best repatriation book I read. The exercises are useful, and the writing is clear and helpful."
—*Danielle Summerlin*

"This workbook is a must for everyone re-entering their home-country or a country they have lived before. Cate Brubaker experienced re-entry herself and guides you through the different stages, helps you reframe your re-entry, understand the process and manage your expectations before and during transition. With simple steps this book helps you and your family address the most important steps of a healthy re-entry. You will define your very own Global Life Ingredients that will make you reframe your perspective on your international life from "being abroad" vs "being at home" to "living a global life" that includes this re-entry as one of the mile markers on your journey."
—*Ute Limacher-Riebold*

TABLE OF CONTENTS

1. Introduction — 15

2. Reflection Activities — 29

3. My Global Life Ingredients — 69

4. My Forward Launch — 91

5. My Re-entry Roadmap — 105

6. Next Steps — 121

7. About the Author — 124

The Re-entry Roadmap

There are FAR, FAR BETTER THINGS ahead THAN ANY we leave behind.

C.S. Lewis

The Re-entry Roadmap

Section 1:
INTRODUCTION

"You will never be completely at home again, because part of your heart always will be elsewhere."

~ Miriam Adeney

WELCOME!

You've had an amazing adventure abroad and now you're thinking about your next steps. Whether you're returning "home" indefinitely, you plan to move abroad again in the future, or something in-between, you have so many options for continuing to live a life of inspired global adventure. The world is still your oyster!

These days the question isn't so much *what* can you do next, but rather what's your *best* next step? That can be a difficult question to answer, especially when you're in the throes of reverse culture shock. The Re-entry Roadmap is here to help! Whether you're still abroad and thinking about your upcoming re-entry, you've just returned, or you've been "home" for several months (or even years), the Re-entry Roadmap will guide you in processing your complex emotions, deeply reflecting on your identity, and fine-tuning your mindset so you can find your best next step—what I call your Forward Launch—that leads to a life you love even more than the one you lived abroad.

The Re-entry Roadmap is perfect for you if you:

- Have lived, worked, taught, interned, studied, volunteered, or traveled abroad.
- Feel changed by your experiences abroad and don't want to simply go back to a life at home that now feels a size too small.
- Are deciding whether to remain in your home country or move abroad again.
- Desire strong relationships, a successful career, and a life of global adventure.
- Seek a meaningful, satisfying, and sustainable global life, no matter where in the world you are.
- Want to feel as alive and engaged at home as you did abroad.
- Would rather prioritize reflection and action over complaining and commiserating.

The Re-entry Roadmap will help you:

- Review your experiences and travels abroad.
- Reflect on what you learned while living abroad and how you've changed.
- Unpack your complex—and often conflicting—emotions.
- Adjust to being home in a way that keeps you moving forward with confidence and connection.
- Create actionable strategies for making re-entry a positive growth experience.
- Incorporate global adventure into your everyday life.
- Clarify what (and who) is truly important to you going forward.
- Identify your Global Life Ingredients and use them as a compass in your life and career.
- Confidently make decisions about your future.
- Find greater insight, meaning, and ease in your re-entry experience.

SO, WHAT *IS* RE-ENTRY, EXACTLY?

Simply put, re-entry is the experience of returning to the place you once called home. It's a physical, mental, and emotional transition. Whether you return "home" for a few weeks for vacation, a couple years in-between stints abroad or you repatriate indefinitely, you'll experience re-entry.

You may have heard the term *reverse culture shock*, which is like the culture shock you felt when you first went abroad. This time, however, you feel frustrated—not to mention surprised!—that everything that was once familiar is suddenly strange and foreign. I see reverse culture shock as an element of re-entry.

Re-entry is about going "home," but it's also about redefining home. It's about gaining a deeper perspective of what "global" means to you and how you want it to show up in your life. It's about getting to know the new you, finding your unique Global Life Ingredients, and deciding on your best next step. Focusing on these things will give you the inspiration, confidence, and connection that you crave after living abroad. With the right approach, re-entry can be a huge opportunity for growth and forward movement that leads to even bigger and better things!

You might feel an unspoken expectation to slip seamlessly back into your old life (I sure did). As if your time abroad—whether weeks, months, or years—was simply a fun side trip, and now it's time to get back to "real" life.

I don't see it that way. The goal of re-entry isn't to simply readjust to the status quo. Even if you wanted to, you couldn't go back to the home you left behind, because that home doesn't exist in the way it did before. Not only have you changed—your friends and family have changed (even if it doesn't seem like it initially). Your community has changed. There's no going back. The only way to go is forward.

Re-entry provides you with a unique opportunity to take a step back, take stock of who you are and what you want your relationships, career, and life to be like *now*, and then intentionally create a meaningful, satisfying, and sustainable global life that you love even more than the life you lived abroad.

THE #1 MISTAKE RETURNEES MAKE

I'm not going to sugarcoat it; re-entry is tough for the vast majority of returnees. For most people it's the absolute hardest part of the entire living abroad experience. You wouldn't think that going *home*, returning to the familiar, would be so difficult, right?

But it is.

Because it's such a difficult transition, the mistake most returnees make is to avoid acknowledging re-entry as a way to cope with it. (I definitely did.) It's a natural response, and it's not surprising that so many of us do this, because going home after being abroad often evokes painful feelings—and it's normal to avoid something that makes you feel bad.

There are all sorts of ways returnees avoid acknowledging the pain of re-entry. They...

- Get really busy with school, work, family, friends, or other commitments.
- Ignore how they're feeling, don't seek out people who can help, and muddle through alone.
- Indulge in things that distract them from their difficult feelings in the short term but don't offer solutions to re-entry challenges in the long run.
- Focus on going abroad again as soon as possible so they can once again feel the euphoria that travel and landing in a new place brings.
- Get on with "real life" and compartmentalize their experiences abroad. They think, "*Well, my time living abroad is over, so why think about it now? I should focus on the future.*"

And when returnees do talk about re-entry? They tend to stick to the "3 Cs": *crying, complaining* about how nobody wants to hear their stories from abroad, and *contemplating* their escape.

Do any of these re-entry coping strategies sound familiar? I'm the first to admit that I've used many of them. But then I figured out a better way.

Before we dive into what that better way is, let's look at a few reasons why returnees so often just want to avoid dealing with re-entry. Do any sound familiar?

First, returnees often see re-entry as not just the end of an experience living abroad but as the end of living an amazing global life. They often feel like they're expected to readjust to a home that they've outgrown, and that feels small and restrictive; they may feel as though they're going backwards.

Second, returnees often hear re-entry and reverse culture shock described like illnesses with numerous negative symptoms. Of course you're going to want to avoid re-entry if it sounds like a sickness you have to struggle through.

Third, re-entry often stirs up deep feelings, and sometimes conflicting ones, about home, language, nationality, belonging, family, career, and what makes us fulfilled and happy. It can also stir up feelings relating to unresolved personal or relationship issues or even old wounds. These emotions can feel overwhelming.

Fourth, re-entry can feel akin to losing a cherished relationship through a breakup or even death. The feelings evoked are similar to what people experience going through the grieving process. The life you built abroad (whether you lived that life for weeks, months, or years) is now over, and that can really, really hurt.

Fifth, returnees often fall into either/or thinking about home vs abroad—namely that the only place where they feel truly happy, adventurous, successful, visible, and special, is abroad. And on the flip slide, being back at home means feeling the opposite: unhappy, bored, failing, and invisible. Especially if you didn't want to return, it's very easy to get stuck in this type of limited thinking.

Sixth, returnees' identity is often wrapped up in being the one who lives abroad, travels the world, speaks other languages, does hard things that others find impressive. You might just not know who you are back at home, or miss who you were abroad. It's common to feel a loss of identity in re-entry.

And, finally, the vast majority of returnees lack meaningful tools, support or guidance through the more challenging aspects of re-entry.

Why? Picture an iceberg. What's interesting about an iceberg is that 90 percent of it is completely invisible, below the water line. So, if you're in a boat floating on the water, you'll only see the top 10 percent. Re-entry is just like an iceberg; most people only see the 10 of the re-entry experience that's easily visible.

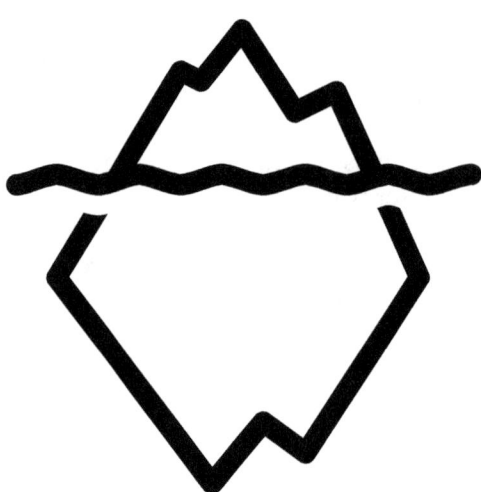

What's in the visible 10 percent of the re-entry iceberg? Things like travel logistics, unpacking, getting over jet lag, updating your resume, creating new routines, reuniting with friends and family, and some elements of reverse culture shock, such as seeing your home country and culture from a new perspective. These are the first aspects of re-entry that returnees encounter, and they share several attributes: they're visible and easy to recognize and talk about, they apply to a large number of returnees, they're typically experienced by returnees on a similar timeline, and they're things returnees most often do receive support for. Additionally, they're not very emotionally charged.

In the 90 percent of the re-entry iceberg that's invisible below the water line you'll find more challenging things like deep grief, feelings of loss, conflicting emotions, difficulty navigating relationships, loss of identity, feelings of not belonging, and much more. These are the elements of re-entry that are internal, invisible, emotionally charged, and often very subtle.

Before we go on, take a moment to think about what's in *your* re-entry iceberg. Jot down your notes below.

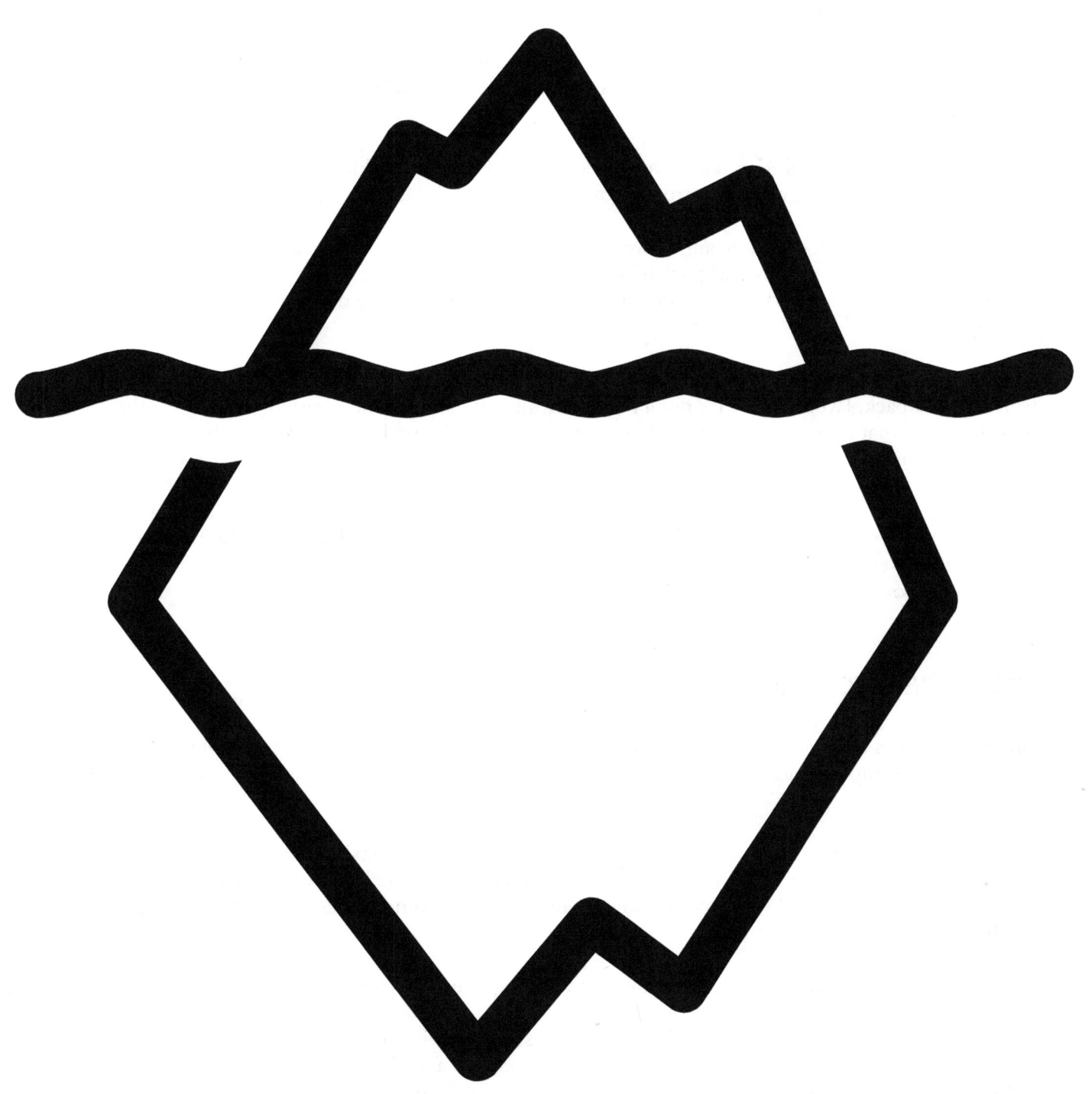

Returnees are typically left to process the much more challenging elements of re-entry completely on their own because they often don't surface until weeks, months, or even years after a return home. What makes it even more challenging is that different elements surface for different returnees, in different intensities, and on different timelines. So it's not surprising that so many returnees choose avoidance as a coping strategy.

But here's what happens if you do.

Picture your favorite travel backpack. Now imagine that a rock is magically added to your backpack each night while you're asleep: one rock for every day you avoid acknowledging re-entry as a way to cope with it.

At first, it's not a big deal. You don't even notice the rocks that are added to your backpack every night. And you actually get a little stronger from carrying all the extra weight around!

But then, as time goes on, more and more rocks are added and your backpack gets heavier and heavier. At some point, your backpack is so full of re-entry rocks that it drags you down and becomes too heavy to carry. Depending on the person, this could take days, weeks, or months (even years).

Each day that you avoid re-entry—whether consciously or unconsciously—you add a rock to your mental backpack. Even though it's not a big deal at first, it can become a very big one down the road. And at that point, you might not have any idea where the rocks came from in the first place, which can make getting rid of them even harder.

The good news is that you don't have to wait until your mental backpack is overflowing with re-entry rocks! If you become aware of what's in your re-entry iceberg and make a habit of deeply processing re-entry after each experience abroad, you won't accumulate these rocks and they won't ever weigh you down. The Re-entry Roadmap helps you do just that.

REST. REFLECT. REFUEL.

Many returnees approach re-entry with significant trepidation, sadness, or even outright fear. Even returnees who moved back to their home country happily often feel constrained, bored, or restless after a while.

Returning "home" can feel like shutting a door on friendships, a lifestyle or an identity that you loved, not to mention all things global. You might find that your life back home feels suffocatingly small. It might feel like you're stuck opening a can of soup for dinner each night after having unlimited access to gourmet meals.

What if you were to reframe re-entry from the very beginning? Perhaps like this…

Imagine you're on a month-long road trip. It's impossible to drive the entire way without stopping, right? That would be crazy and dangerous. So, every once in a while you pull into a rest area to stretch your legs, check your navigation, and get a cup of coffee.

Even though you're not moving forward toward your destination, do you worry that your road trip is over? Or that you'll get stuck at the rest area?

Of course not!

You simply rest, reflect, and refuel, because that's what rest areas are for, and you know that taking a break is what will enable you to continue your journey and reach your destination.

Now imagine that you reluctantly stopped at that rest area, left your car idling, and sat uncomfortably in the driver's seat for a couple hours while thinking about the highway you wish you were driving on, while commiserating with your travel companions about having to spend all that time in the rest area. All because you're afraid that getting out of the car means your road trip will end.

Sounds crazy, right?

But that's exactly how many returnees approach re-entry after living abroad! They return home physically but are mentally still abroad, they worry that their global life has come to an end, and they commiserate with others who feel the exact same way.

When you're on a road trip you don't fear the rest area. Rather, you welcome it because you know that what the rest area offers—a place (and time) to stretch your legs, check your navigation, and get a cup of coffee—is exactly what you need to keep moving forward toward your destination, once you're ready to get back on the road.

So, what if you were to adopt the same outlook on re-entry? What if you were to look at re-entry as a rest area that provides you with a place to rest, reflect, and refuel after your experiences abroad? A place where you can stay as long as you want and leave whenever you feel ready. A place that exists to help you keep moving forward.

The Re-entry Roadmap is your rest area guide. It will help you rest, reflect, refuel, and then continue on your lifelong global journey.

MY RE-ENTRY STORY

So that you know where I'm coming from, and why I created the Re-entry Roadmap, here's my own (very much abridged) re-entry story.

My first re-entry was at 17 years old, after spending my senior year of high school as an exchange student in Germany.

It was rocky, to say the least!

I wasn't especially happy to be back home. Once the novelty of seeing my family and friends wore off, I longed for the life I'd worked so hard to build in Germany. I missed speaking German every day, I craved the daily adventure of living abroad (and living in a big city), and I struggled to navigate the weird distance that appeared in what had been my closest relationships with family and friends at home.

It was disheartening that the person I'd become seemed largely invisible to everyone but me. I deeply questioned where I belonged. I wanted both "home roots" and "global wings"—but I wanted to define and live them on *my* terms.

I muddled through as best I could until I moved abroad again a few years later. As a highly introspective person, I automatically thought a lot about what I'd learned and how living abroad had changed me. But I had no tools for doing anything productive with all that reflection, and it just sat at the not-very-helpful level of vague awareness for several years.

And the overflow of conflicting emotions that I felt throughout my entire body but couldn't articulate? I had no idea how to process all of that, and probably took it out on my loved ones more than I intended.

I rebelled against the pressure I felt to return to "real life" (as if living abroad isn't real life?) and readjust back to what I'd left. To me, readjusting felt like going backwards. I felt like my experiences abroad and big, important parts of my identity were being erased. I wanted strong relationships at home but I also wanted to keep moving forward as the person I'd become. I wanted to feel authentically and globally me, no matter where in the world I landed.

I read a couple re-entry books and attended the few workshops available to me. They made me feel like I wasn't crazy! And I enjoyed being around other returnees who understood what I was going through on a cellular level. But the information was relatively superficial and only helped to a point, and we often just ended up commiserating about everything we didn't like about being home, which made me (and probably many others) feel even worse.

Fast-forward nearly two decades after that first re-entry. By this time I'd experienced re-entry several times, in several different ways, at different ages, solo and with other people, and returning to various locations in my home country. After stumbling through my own multiple re-entries, and seeing so many other globetrotters do the same, I decided to find a better way for us all.

Grad school and my career in international education afforded me a deep understanding of the research on transitions, reverse culture shock, re-entry/repatriation, and meaningful reflection, and added to my knowledge gained from years of hands-on experience helping global travelers before, during, and after living abroad.

I became fascinated by the unique and untapped opportunity for growth that re-entry offered. I realized that we were limiting ourselves with the way many of us viewed and approached re-entry, so I set out to create a new approach. One that inspires returnees to navigate going home with greater insight and meaning. One that's more positive than negative. One that, while not always easy, results in significant growth. One that returnees significantly benefit from.

The tools I initially created started out as a way for me to finally reflect on my own experiences abroad and my own re-entries in a meaningful and productive way. When I shared my story and creative approach with friends and colleagues, they encouraged me to share my materials more widely—and the Re-entry Roadmap (and SmallPlanetStudio.com) was born.

THE RE-ENTRY ROADMAP PROCESS

The goal of the five-step Re-entry Roadmap is to help you discover who you are and what you want your life to be like now, so you can find greater insight, meaning, and ease in your return and move forward with confidence and connection. This workbook leads you through a series of reflective activities designed to help you:

1. **Identify your emotions.**
    You'll process your complex emotions about your experiences abroad and returning "home"— *so you can feel calm and centered instead of stressed, overwhelmed, and alienated.*

2. **Reframe re-entry.**
    You'll fine-tune your re-entry mindset—*so you can feel confident, connected, and prepared for what's next.*

3. **Unpack your re-entry backpack.**
    You'll take those re-entry rocks out of your backpack by reflecting on what you learned abroad as well as who you are and what you want your life to be like now—*so you can feel deliciously global, alive, and adventurous on your terms no matter where you are.*

4. **Pinpoint your Global Life Ingredients.**
    You'll redefine "home" and "global" and create strategies for being "home" in a way that keeps you moving forward—*so you can strengthen both your "home roots" and your "global wings."*

5. **Create your Forward Launch.**
    You'll use the insight gained through your deep reflection to find your best next step—*so you can feel excited about what's next for you, you and your partner, or you and your family.*

IS THE RE-ENTRY ROADMAP AN ACTUAL MAP?

Yes! The Re-entry Roadmap is a set of seven pages that create a map that illustrates your personal journey, from your return home to your Forward Launch (you'll find it at the end of this workbook). It looks like this:

As you work through the activities in this book, you'll complete each of the seven roadmap pages. Once you've finished the workbook, you'll have a personalized roadmap to hang on your wall and remind yourself where you've been and where you're going.

Notice that the roadmap pages are black and white? The Re-entry Roadmap is meant to be creative, fun, and inspiring, so grab your favorite art supplies and personalize it. Enjoy the process!

HOW TO USE THE RE-ENTRY ROADMAP

You've made the investment to purchase the Re-entry Roadmap, and I want to make sure you get the most out of the process. Here are seven tips to get you started:

1. Gather your favorite supplies. You're going to do a lot of writing, so grab the pens that make you happy!

2. Find some alone time. It's hard to reflect when your attention is being pulled elsewhere, so find a space and some time where you won't be interrupted (even if it's just for 10 minutes at a time). Turn off your phone and leave your laptop and iPad in the other room. Lower the volume on the distractions around you so you can hear your inner self.

3. Create a comfortable space for reflection. For me, that's sitting on my deck with an iced coffee and often a cat in my lap. What kind of environment feeds your inspiration?

4. Do what feels right. There are many activities in this workbook; do the ones that speak to you. I recommend completing the exercises in the order in which they appear in the workbook, as they do build on each other. That said, they'll still make sense if you do them in a different order.

5. Connect with others. If you're going through re-entry with a friend, partner, your family or as a cohort, consider going through this workbook together. Better yet, join our Re-entry Roadmap Facebook group or one of our small group or coaching programs. You'll find more information about these options at https://smallplanetstudio.com/rr-bonus

6. Take your time. You don't have to complete the entire workbook in one go! It's actually better to give yourself time and space for reflection and processing. Find the right pace for you.

7. Don't stop. The activities—especially the ones towards the beginning—can stir up a lot of emotions, and you may find it overwhelming to process everything. My best advice is to take a break…and then keep going. These activities lay the groundwork for identifying your Global Life Ingredients and finding your best next step, and those are two things you don't want to miss!

DON'T FORGET YOUR FREE BONUSES

Visit https://smallplanetstudio.com/rr-bonus for more re-entry resources!

WHAT DO I WANT TO ACCOMPLISH?

What do you want to accomplish by following the Re-entry Roadmap? Check all that apply below.

I want to…

____ Process how I feel about re-entry, transitions, and being home.

____ Fine-tune my mindset so re-entry becomes something I grow and benefit from.

____ Create strategies that help me adjust forward and thrive in re-entry.

____ Strengthen both my "home roots" and my "global wings."

____ Reflect on my identity—who I am *now*—and what I want my life to be like going forward.

____ Pinpoint my Global Life Ingredients so I can create my Forward Launch with confidence.

____ Live a global life that's even better than the one I lived abroad.

____ Other: _____

READY TO GET STARTED?

Maybe you studied, volunteered, interned or taught abroad. Perhaps you moved your family to a new country for your or your partner's job. Maybe you wandered the world for weeks, months, or even years on end. Whatever your reason for being abroad, you're now facing a brand-new challenge: going "home."

You went abroad because you're curious. You seek adventure! You're dissatisfied with the status quo, and you want to learn, challenge yourself, and grow. Your eyes have been opened to new ideas, languages, and ways of doing things. Not only that, you've been bitten—hard—by the travel bug. In short, you've been forever, completely, and utterly changed.

Now back home, you're sad that your amazing experience abroad is over. You wonder, *"What's next? Will my future be as good as my past?"* And some days, all you really want to do is catch the next flight to…anywhere.

You might assume that your global adventure is over, but rest assured that "home" is where the real adventure begins. Travel is the catalyst; re-entry is where transformation is made visible.

Let the adventure begin!

Section 2: REFLECTION ACTIVITIES

> *"When everything seems to be going against you, remember that the airplane takes off against the wind, not with it."*
> ~ Henry Ford

This section of the Re-entry Roadmap is all about processing your emotions, reflecting on your identity, and fine-tuning your mindset so you can adjust to being home in a way that keeps your relationships, life, and career moving forward. The reflection activities in this section lay the groundwork for pinpointing your Global Life Ingredients and identifying your best next step—your Forward Launch—later in the workbook.

The activities in this section can evoke all sorts of feelings. Readers have said they can be emotionally taxing…but so worth the effort. As one returnee put it, it's like chopping onions. First they make you cry, then they make a delicious meal. Pace yourself, take breaks when needed, practice self-care, connect with me and the Small Planet Studio Facebook group for support, and keep going. Your future self will thank you!

WHY IS RE-ENTRY SO F*@!ING HARD?

Are you finding re-entry more difficult than expected? You're not alone! Whether soon after arrival or months later, most returnees are surprised to find a whole lot more bumps on the re-entry road than they expected. Remember the re-entry iceberg? Those "below-the-waterline" elements of re-entry are beginning to surface!

You might be wondering why we're starting with an activity about why re-entry is so difficult, given that this workbook is intended to be positive, optimistic, and upbeat. While I want to help you make re-entry a positive experience, I don't want to sugarcoat anything. This is hard! You're going through a major life transition that most people around you just don't understand.

Rather than negativity, we're starting with *honesty* about the re-entry experience. This activity will help you articulate what you find most challenging, which will help you explain your struggles to others (should you wish to), develop a strong support system, and create effective strategies for thriving in re-entry (we'll get to the latter two topics a bit later in the workbook).

On the next page you'll find 25 reasons why re-entry can be such a challenge. Circle the ones that are true for you.

25 REASONS WHY RE-ENTRY IS SO HARD

1. Home no longer feels like home. In fact, I'm not even sure what "home" is anymore.
2. I miss the lifestyle, weather, food, or circle of friends I had abroad.
3. I thought re-entry was just those first couple weeks adjusting to jet lag and driving my car again; I had no idea it would hit me on a deeper and more intense level several weeks or months after arriving home.
4. I'm frustrated that while I've been significantly changed by my experiences abroad, I can't seem to articulate exactly how I've changed when talking with family, friends or prospective employers.
5. Even though I'm physically home, if I'm really honest, I'm mentally still abroad.
6. I feel like nobody at home sees who I am now. They only see the person I was before I went abroad.
7. I only heard terrible, horrible things about re-entry, and so I expected it to be a terrible, horrible experience (and it has been).
8. My re-entry experience has been somewhat different from my friends', partner's or family's, and now I'm wondering if there's something wrong with me.
9. I feel like I have to settle or give up things or people that are important to me in order to have the global life I want.
10. Whereas going abroad was a largely external experience that I could share via social media, emails, and photos, re-entry is largely internal. I'm finding that it's much more difficult to share my re-entry ups and downs with others, especially if they haven't been through it themselves.
11. I've been through re-entry before and didn't struggle with it, and so I'm surprised that it's more difficult this time around.
12. I no longer feel "special" as the expat, study abroad student, volunteer, etc. I miss feeling special in that way.
13. Being abroad felt like moving forward. Being back home feels like stagnating or even going backwards.
14. Re-entry is shining a spotlight on personal issues I struggle with.
15. I didn't completely fit in with my host culture while abroad, and now I don't feel like I fit in with my home culture. I'm not sure where I belong.
16. I'm going through re-entry alone and I feel isolated and lonely.
17. People assume that living abroad was simply a phase, and that now that I'm back I'll return to "real life." I'm frustrated that they don't realize that being abroad *was* real life.
18. I haven't received any re-entry support. I feel like I'm in a sink-or-swim situation.
19. I thought I knew who I was, but now I'm not so sure.
20. Re-entry washes over me at unexpected times and is triggered by unexpected things. I never know when it's going to reappear and make me feel miserable.

21. I'm worried that my studies or career will stall.
22. Being back home seems incredibly boring. I worry I'm losing my sense of adventure.
23. I want to go abroad again, but I'm not sure how to make that happen.
24. I feel out of sync with friends and family.
25. I don't know what to do next with my life and I worry about getting stuck.

Every time I read through this list I still feel *so many feelings*! I originally listed these 25 reasons on the Small Planet Studio blog, and then asked my Twitter friends if they had more to add. They sure did! And I bet you do, too.

Jot down *your* reasons why re-entry is so hard in the space below. Include everything you can think of, big, or small.

Now that you've identified what you find difficult about re-entry, you can create strategies that will help you thrive. The rest of the Re-entry Roadmap will help you do just that.

HOW DO I FEEL? HOW DO I *WANT* TO FEEL?

Feelings. Returning home after living abroad brings up so many of them! Your feelings are important to listen to because they're data that tell you what you want and don't want in your life going forward. They help you create healthy boundaries and articulate your dreams and desires, and they'll guide you in finding your best next step after living abroad. They're also the starting point for your own Re-entry Roadmap (which you'll find at the end of this workbook).

To begin, take a look at the Feelings List on the next page. Use a pen to circle the words that describe how you're currently feeling. Then use a highlighter (or different colored pen) for the words that represent how you *want* to feel. If you don't see what you're currently feeling or what you want to feel in the Feelings List, add them.

Then, answer the discovery questions on the following page.

You may wish to keep track of your re-entry feelings in a journal or planner, so you can reflect on the events, people, and activities in your life that help or hinder you in feeling how you want to feel. If you'd like to see how other returnees feel in re-entry, take a look at our bonus resources page at https://smallplanetstudio.com/rr-bonus

I want to stress here that it can be helpful in re-entry to talk with a professional. Whether you choose a re-entry coach, a counselor, or a therapist specializing in global transitions, professional and individualized attention might be exactly what you need to move forward. If you think you could benefit from working with a coach or a therapist, check the resources I've listed in the online bonus section (see link above).

"Happiness is not something readymade. It comes from your own actions."

~ Dalai Lama

FEELINGS LIST

- agonized
- alarmed
- alert
- alive
- alone
- amazed
- ambitious
- amused
- angry
- annoyed
- anticipating
- anxious
- appalled
- appreciated
- apprehensive
- at ease
- baffled
- benevolent
- bewildered
- bitter
- bold
- bored
- brave
- capable
- cared for
- certain
- challenged
- cheerful
- comfortable
- comforted
- concerned
- confident
- confused
- consoled
- content
- courageous
- crushed
- cynical
- curious
- daring
- delighted
- dependent
- desperate
- determined
- disappointed
- discontented
- disinterested
- dismayed
- disoriented
- dissatisfied
- drained
- eager
- embarrassed
- empathic
- energetic
- energized
- enthusiastic
- envious
- ecstatic
- excited
- exhausted
- fearful
- fed up
- fired up
- forlorn
- free
- friendly
- frustrated
- glad
- gloomy
- graceful
- guilty
- happy
- helpless
- heartbroken
- hopeful
- hopeless
- horrified
- hurt
- impatient
- impotent
- important
- impulsive
- inadequate
- independent
- indifferent
- ineffectual
- inspired
- intelligent
- inventive
- irritated
- joyful
- lethargic
- left out
- liberated
- lonely
- lost
- loved
- mad
- miserable
- misplaced
- mixed up
- moody
- motivated
- nervous
- optimistic
- overjoyed
- overwhelmed
- panicked
- patient
- peaceful
- pitied
- playful
- proud
- provoked
- reassured
- rebellious
- receptive
- regretful
- rejected
- relieved
- reluctant
- resentful
- resigned
- respected
- restless
- sad
- satisfied
- secure
- self-conscious
- sensitive
- serene
- shocked
- sick
- small
- spontaneous
- strong
- stuck
- sulky
- suspicious
- sympathetic
- tenacious
- tense
- terrified
- timid
- tired
- torn
- trapped
- uncomfortable
- undecided
- uneasy
- unhappy
- unimportant
- unique
- unloved
- unpopular
- unsure
- upset
- vibrant
- wanted
- warm
- wearied
- weary
- worn out
- worried
- worthy
- yearning
- zealous

The Re-entry Roadmap

HOW I CURRENTLY FEEL	HOW I WANT TO FEEL

WHEN & WHERE DO I FEEL THESE EMOTIONS?

WHAT ARE THREE THINGS I CAN DO EACH DAY TO FEEL THE WAY I WANT TO FEEL?

1.

2.

3.

MY CONFLICTING EMOTIONS

As you surveyed the Feelings List did you find that you have a lot of mixed emotions? If so, you're not alone. It's ok—even expected—to have wildly conflicting feelings in re-entry! Returnees often assume it means they're doing something wrong but I want to assure you that it's completely normal. So, instead of ignoring them, let's name them. Instead of judging your emotions, let's get curious. Instead of fighting them, let's own them!

Start by first listing your conflicting feelings below. Then answer the discovery questions on the next page.

I FEEL　　　　　　　　　　　　　　　　　**I FEEL**

	AND	
	AND	
	AND	
	AND	
	AND	

Remember, *it's ok* that to feel all of these conflicting emotions at once!

HOW DO I TYPICALLY REACT WHEN I FEEL CONFLICTING EMOTIONS?	WHAT DO I NOTICE ABOUT MYSELF WHEN I FEEL CONFLICTING EMOTIONS?
WHAT ARE THESE CONFLICTING EMOTIONS TEACHING ME?	HOW WOULD MY RE-ENTRY CHANGE IF I SIMPLY ACCEPTED THESE CONFLICTING EMOTIONS?

MY ASSUMPTIONS ABOUT RE-ENTRY

The way you perceive re-entry affects the way you experience it. This activity gives you the opportunity to explore your assumptions of and perceptions about the re-entry transition. In the space below, write down everything that comes to you when you think about re-entry.

Now take a look at what you listed above. Circle the words that are positive and underline the negative ones. Which do you have more of: positive or negative? (Spoiler alert: most returnees find that their assumptions and perceptions skew negative.) Now answer the reflection questions below.

HOW DO THE THINGS I LISTED ABOVE HELP ME?	**HOW DO THE THINGS I LISTED ABOVE HINDER ME?**

REFRAMING RE-ENTRY

One way to make re-entry a more positive experience is to figure out how to see the positive in it. I'm not suggesting you ignore the difficult parts, but rather that you reframe re-entry into something that's more appealing to you. You'll then be in a more positive and productive state of mind, which makes you more open to opportunities, connections, and growth, as well as happier overall.

As I mentioned earlier, I like to think of re-entry as a *rest area* that gives me the opportunity to rest, reflect, and refuel before continuing on my life-long global journey. If that reframe works for you, too, great! If not, here's your opportunity to create your own re-entry reframe.

Start by brainstorming all of the tangible and intangible things you find positive, inspirational, enjoyable or motivational. Write your list below.

Now, choose something from your brainstorm list and complete the sentence below to create your re-entry reframe:

I used to think of re-entry as a/an _____,

but because I want a positive re-entry experience, I'm going to reframe re-entry and think of it as a/

an _____, because

_____.

Two things to note:

- If you don't find a reframe that works for you right away, don't worry. Give it time; it will come to you.

- If creating a reframe for re-entry just doesn't work for you, that's ok! As one returnee told me, she prefers to just "call a spade a spade."

What to do with your re-entry reframe? Write it in your planner or journal, make it the background image on your computer or phone, add it to your vision board, jot it on a sticky note and place it on your bathroom mirror, tattoo it on your wrist (ok, maybe not…or maybe?).

The main thing is to keep your re-entry reframe front and center when you return home so it can guide you in creating a positive, growth-focused transition that leads to even bigger and better things.

Tip: You know how some people choose a word as their theme for the year? Why not make your re-entry reframe your word(s) for the year (or rest of the year, depending on when you're doing this exercise)?

> "{Fellow returnees} sing a song only you can hear."
>
> ~ Oscar Wilde

POSITIVE AND NEGATIVE

While you don't want to wallow in negativity, it helps to be honest about how you're feeling. Expressing your emotions will lead to more growth than staying quiet about them. So for the next five minutes, you're going to engage in mindful venting. This is your opportunity to get everything that you dislike about re-entry, transitions, and being back home off your chest.

Grab a pen and set a timer for five minutes. In the space below, write down every single thing you dislike about re-entry, transitions, and being back home. Include *everything* that comes to you! You can always rip this page out of the workbook and shred it if you don't want anyone to see your venting.

If you're doing this activity with a friend, your partner, or as a family, why not make it a friendly competition? See who can come up with the longest list!

Feel better? Sometimes a few minutes of mindful venting can do so much good. Now take a few minutes to reflect on what you wrote using the discovery questions below.

HOW DID I FEEL AS I MADE MY LIST?	HOW DID IT FEEL TO ACKNOWLEDGE THE NEGATIVE ASPECTS OF RE-ENTRY?

WHAT AM I LEARNING ABOUT MYSELF BY WRITING DOWN THE NEGATIVE ASPECTS OF RE-ENTRY?

Now, let's look at the brighter side. In the space below, list all the things that are good about re-entry, transitions, and being back home. It might be difficult at first, but I bet you can think of at least a few! Refer to this list frequently, to remind yourself that being back home isn't *all* bad.

FINDING BALANCE

When I was a kid, my mom made a roast chicken at least twice a week. I didn't dislike it, but it wasn't my favorite dinner, and I often complained about it (sorry, Mom).

A few months after I moved to Germany as a teen I was surprised by how much I missed my mom's roast chicken! I'm pretty sure I dreamt about it at least once. The thing is, I could have roasted a chicken if I'd really wanted to, but I never did. My hankering was more nostalgia, homesickness, and wanting a hug from my mom than an actual desire for a particular food. I knew that if I were back home, I'd complain as soon as I saw chicken on the dinner table.

I share this story because nostalgia is powerful. Faced with the reality of being back home, it's easy to glamorize "abroad" in our mind and conveniently forget about all those not-so-wonderful aspects of daily life there. Likewise, it's easy to take the positive aspects of home for granted and instead become focused on the less-than-satisfactory elements.

That's why this activity is meant to help you find balance between reality and nostalgia for both where you were abroad and where you are now.

The first step is to write down all of the things you liked and disliked about where you were and what you like and dislike about where you are now. Then answer the corresponding discovery questions.

"When one door of happiness closes, another opens, but often we look so long at the closed door that we do not see the one that has been opened for us!"

~ Helen Keller

The Re-entry Roadmap

**WHAT I LIKED ABOUT
WHERE I WAS ABROAD**

**WHAT I LIKE ABOUT
WHERE I AM NOW**

**WHAT I DISLIKED ABOUT
WHERE I WAS ABROAD**

**WHAT I DISLIKE ABOUT
WHERE I AM NOW**

The Re-entry Roadmap

WHAT SIMILARITIES DO I SEE BETWEEN WHAT I LIKED ABOUT WHERE I WAS ABROAD AND WHERE I AM NOW?

HOW CAN I INTEGRATE WHAT I LIKED ABOUT BEING ABROAD INTO MY LIFE NOW?

WHAT SIMILARITIES DO I SEE BETWEEN WHAT I DISLIKED ABOUT WHERE I WAS ABROAD AND WHERE I AM NOW?

HOW CAN I INTEGRATE WHAT I LIKE ABOUT WHERE I AM NOW INTO MY NEXT STEP?

WHAT GIVES ME HOME ROOTS?

WHAT GIVES ME GLOBAL WINGS?

COPING OR THRIVING?

If you've been home for more than a few days, you've probably already developed some re-entry coping strategies. This activity offers you an opportunity to decide whether these coping strategies are helping or hindering your growth and ability to adjust in a way that keeps you moving forward with confidence and connection.

Here's an example. When you feel misunderstood by friends and family, you might retreat to your bedroom and fire up Netflix. Or, when you feel sad about no longer being abroad, you might jump on social media in order to reconnect with friends who shared your global experiences.

Either strategy can be positive or negative. Watching Netflix, for example, could be the perfect time-out. Or it could be a way to numb yourself to difficult feelings. Connecting with friends on social could be a way to feel seen and understood. Or it could be a way to avoid the reality that your experience abroad has come to a close and it's time to embark on your next adventure.

In this next activity, you'll take stock of your current coping strategies and evaluate how they're working for you. Then, you'll choose and refine the best ones to draw on in the future.

To begin, list all the ways you currently cope with re-entry—big and small, positive and negative, helpful and hindering. Do you stay really busy? Go for a walk in nature each day? Eat too much or too little? Write everything down below.

Now circle the strategies that help you adjust *forward* and underline the ones that hinder you. Which do you have more of? How satisfied are you with your current re-entry coping strategies? If you're happy with them, that's great! If not, let's make them work better for you.

Let's start by looking back at the activity on page 36. Review how you answered the questions, *How do I feel* and *How do I want to feel?* Then answer the reflection questions below.

IN WHAT WAYS DO MY CURRENT COPING STRATEGIES HELP ME FEEL THE WAY I WANT TO FEEL?	IN WHAT WAYS DO MY CURRENT COPING STRATEGIES HINDER MY ABILITY TO FEEL THE WAY I WANT TO?

Now that you've identified the things that help you feel the way you want to feel, let's look more closely at a few of your current coping strategies so you can make them work better for you. Use the reflection on the following page.

The Re-entry Roadmap

When I feel…
_____

I tend to cope by
_____
_____

When I do this, it makes me feel
_____

Here's how I can modify this coping strategy
_____
_____

When I feel…
_____

I tend to cope by
_____
_____

When I do this, it makes me feel
_____

Here's how I can modify this coping strategy
_____
_____

When I feel…
_____

I tend to cope by
_____
_____

When I do this, it makes me feel
_____

Here's how I can modify this coping strategy
_____
_____

When I feel…
_____

I tend to cope by
_____
_____

When I do this, it makes me feel
_____

Here's how I can modify this coping strategy
_____
_____

MY STRATEGIES FOR THRIVING IN RE-ENTRY

In the space below, list the strategies that will help you feel the way you want to feel in re-entry. These are your personal strategies for thriving in re-entry. Refer to this page frequently!

RELATIONSHIPS CHECK-IN

Relationships—both with those at home and abroad—change in re-entry. That's why it's helpful to evaluate your relationships with family, friends, colleagues, and even the groups you're part of. This activity helps you do just that.

Use the space below to write about your relationships or at least jot down a few notes. Here are some reflection questions to get you started:

- How have my relationships changed since returning home?
- How do I feel about that change?
- Which relationships currently sustain me?
- Which do I currently find draining?
- What am I grateful for when it comes to my relationships?
- What am I missing from my relationships?

Then answer the discovery questions on the following page.

RELATIONSHIPS I WANT TO PRIORITIZE AND NURTURE	**RELATIONSHIPS I WANT TO PUT ON THE BACK BURNER (FOR NOW)**
RELATIONSHIPS I AM WILLING TO LET GO OF	**MY RELATIONSHIP BOUNDARIES**

MY RE-ENTRY SUPPORT ECOSYSTEM

One of the ways we often cope in re-entry is by relying on a few close friends or family members to meet all of our emotional needs. Not only is that placing a lot of pressure on these who mean the most to us, it also sets us up for disappointment if friends and family don't respond in the way we need or expect.

Here's an alternative: Create an intentional re-entry support ecosystem. If you have a *network* of support, you'll know exactly who to go to when you need a boost, and you'll be more likely to get the support you need, which will help you thrive in re-entry and afterwards.

To create your support ecosystem, start by identifying your needs. Some common re-entry needs are listed below, but be sure to add yours to the list.

venting	travel talk	fun	career advice
laughter	hugs	connection	confiding
adventure	comfort	dreaming	brainstorming

WHAT I NEED IN RE-ENTRY:

Next, list potential sources of support. Write down everyone you can think of—friends, family, colleagues, acquaintances, professors, therapists, coaches, local communities, online groups, websites, blogs, activities, hobbies, Netflix, etc. Support can come in a variety of shapes and sizes!

SOURCES OF SUPPORT:

Now that you've identified your re-entry needs and your avenues of support, it's time to create your personal Re-Entry Support Ecosystem. If you write out your sources of support, you're more likely to remember them! Take a look at the following examples, and then write your own below.

When I want *to connect with other returnees who get what I'm going through,* I'll post in *the Re-entry Roadmap Facebook group.*

When I *miss my life abroad,* I'll *watch my favorite comedy series from my host country on Netflix.*

When *I'm feeling down,* I'll *contact my sister* because I always feel more upbeat and connected after we chat.

The final step? Make use of your support system. Don't suffer in silence!

MY ADVENTURE PASSPORT

Now that you've reflected on many re-entry challenges, let's talk about something more positive, not to mention fun: new experiences and adventures!

One of the best ways to thrive in re-entry is to intentionally seek out new adventures. Whether you're home for a few weeks, several months, or indefinitely, creating an Adventure Passport will prevent you from falling into a re-entry rut.

Start by reflecting on what made you feel "alive" while abroad. Was it certain activities? Being with specific people? Learning new things? In the space below, write down everything that you loved doing while abroad.

Now write down all the things you're looking forward to doing at home, whether for the first or the hundredth time. Maybe you can't wait to revisit a favorite hangout with friends. Perhaps you're eager to connect with local Mandarin speakers. Or maybe you want to take SCUBA lessons in preparation for your next global adventure. Jot it all down below.

The next step is to select 5–10 adventures that you want to have while at home. Make it official by listing them on the next page. Here are a few tips for making the most of your Adventure Passport.

- Set a date for each adventure, and then put it in your calendar. Make these adventures a priority!

- If you're going through re-entry with friends, a partner, or as a family, have everyone share the adventures that they most want to have while at home. Cheer each other on as you complete each one.

- If you're crafty, why not create a simple "passport" out of a pocket journal or small notebook? Write each adventure on a different page in the journal. As you complete each one, jot down notes and memories.

- Once you've completed an adventure, "stamp" your Adventure Passport so you can keep track of your experiences. A simple check mark will do, but why not get creative with gold stars, stickers, or a fun stamp?

Happy adventuring!

"Be not afraid of going slowly, be afraid only of standing still."

~ Chinese Proverb

The Re-entry Roadmap

ADVENTURE	DATE	NOTES / STAMP

WHY I WENT ABROAD

Returnees often find it difficult to articulate how significantly they've grown and changed as a result of being abroad. This activity will help with that by guiding you in reflecting on why you went abroad, what you were hoping to achieve (even if you only realize it in hindsight) and what you did achieve, and then thinking about what you'll do differently next time. Complete the chart below, then answer the reflection questions on the next page.

WHAT I HOPED TO ACHIEVE ABROAD	WHAT I ACHIEVED ABROAD

PERSONALLY

EDUCATIONALLY

PROFESSIONALLY

OTHER

The Re-entry Roadmap

TO WHAT DEGREE DID I ACHIEVE WHAT I WANTED

WHAT DO I WISH I'D DONE DIFFERENTLY WHILE ABROAD?

WHAT DID I NOT ACHIEVE? WHAT FACTORS PLAYED A ROLE IN NOT ACHIEVING THESE THINGS?

IF I GO ABROAD AGAIN, WHAT WILL I DO DIFFERENTLY?

MEET THE NEW YOU

Returnees typically feel like their experiences abroad have changed them, sometimes a great deal—but they often find it hard to articulate exactly *how* they've changed. This activity will help you identify who you are now, as compared to who you were before you went abroad or while you were there. When *you* get clear on the ways you've grown and changed, the easier it is for others to see that growth and change in you.

Use the following three pages to describe:

1. Who you were *before* you went abroad.
2. Who you were *while* abroad.
3. Who you are *now*.

On each page, write down any and all of the words, phrases, or feelings that describe you at these three points in time. You can make a list, draw or simply free-write until you fill the page. Then, go back and highlight the words and phrases that are most meaningful to you as they relate to your identity. Then complete the discovery questions.

Need some help getting started? Try these prompts:

Every day I…	I learn(ed)…
I wish(ed)…	I spend/spent time with…
I love(d)…	I worry(ied) about…
I rarely…	I feel/felt…
I often…	I want(ed)…
I dream(ed) about…	I don't/didn't want…
I wonder(ed)…	I enjoy(ed)…
I think/thought…	I know/knew…

BEFORE I WENT ABROAD I...

WHILE I WAS ABROAD I...

NOW THAT I'VE RETURNED, I...

The Re-entry Roadmap

HOW HAVE I CHANGED OVER TIME?

HOW AM I THE STILL THE SAME?

WHAT PRIVILEGES DO I HAVE THAT I DIDN'T RECOGNIZE UNTIL NOW?

WHAT PART(S) OF MY IDENTITY AM I NOW MORE AWARE OF?

WHAT AM I LEARNING ABOUT MYSELF?

GOODBYE AND HELLO

In order to make room for new opportunities, perspectives, and adventures, it's necessary to let go of what no longer serves you. Before we wrap up the reflection activities and move on to finding your Global Life Ingredients, take a moment to list the attitudes, relationships, coping strategies, and anything else that you're ready to let go of as you move through re-entry and create your Forward Launch. Then, list what you're ready to welcome as you move forward!

WHAT I'M READY TO LET GO OF	WHAT I'M READY TO WELCOME

WRAP UP: ALL ABOUT ME

You made it! This is the final reflection activity. Now it's time to bring everything together by telling your re-entry story. Complete the sentences below.

I spent _____ days/months/years (circle one) in _____.

While there, I liked _____ and _____

but disliked _____ and _____.

Now that I'm home, I appreciate _____ and

_____ but I don't like _____

and _____. Being abroad taught me

_____

_____.

I used to be _____ and _____.

Now I'm _____ and _____. I plan to

draw on _____ and _____ when I need

support, and I'm looking forward to new adventures like _____ and

_____. To make re-entry a positive experience, I'm going to

_____, _____, and

_____. I'm now feeling _____ about

the re-entry experience and how I'm moving forward!

Congratulations—you're ready to find your Global Life Ingredients
and then use them to create your Forward Launch!

The Re-entry Roadmap

Section 3: My GLOBAL LIFE INGREDIENTS

> *"Discovery consists not in seeking new lands but in seeing with new eyes."*
>
> ~ Marcel Proust

You've reflected on your emotions, mindset, and identity in re-entry. In this section, you'll identify your Global Life Ingredients so you can use them as a compass for finding your best next step—what I call your Forward Launch. Let's get started!

WHAT ARE GLOBAL LIFE INGREDIENTS?

Your Global Life Ingredients are a shortlist of things (e.g., people, items, experiences, groups, ideals, feelings, etc.) that you *must* have around you to feel like you're living a meaningful, satisfying, and sustainable global life, no matter where in the world you live.

Your Global Life Ingredients help you:

- Identify your priorities.
- Make important life decisions in re-entry.
- Stay focused on your most meaningful life goals and relationships.
- Find your best next step after living abroad.
- See beyond the outdated and limiting "home vs. abroad" dichotomy.
- Strengthen your "home roots" *and* your "global wings" on your terms.
- Make intentional choices that align with who you are now.
- Feel inspired, confident, and connected, no matter where in the world you are.
- Find meaning and satisfaction in your daily life.

WHAT'S A GLOBAL LIFE?

Ultimately, you'll be the one to decide how you define "a global life," but for now, let's use these parameters so we're on the same page. A global life is one that...

- Reflects who you are now (not who you used to be or who others think you are).
- Builds on what you experienced and learned abroad.
- Doesn't require you to give up the things (or people) that are most important to you.
- Satisfies you, even when it's not easy.
- Incorporates global languages, cultures, people, and perspectives.
- Can be lived just as well in your home country or abroad (or both!).
- Makes you want to jump out of bed in the morning, no matter where in the world you are.
- Is defined and lived on your terms.
- Fits who you are now—and gives you room to grow.

Once you're clear about your Global Life Ingredients, your best next step will become clearer, because you'll know exactly what you need and want to be fulfilled and satisfied going forward.

HOW GLOBAL LIFE INGREDIENTS HELPED ME

My husband, Aaron, and I had always been on the same page when it came to travel, where we wanted to live, and all things global…until one day when we suddenly find ourselves wanting the exact opposite things.

Because we'd enjoyed living abroad, had so much fun traveling together during two career breaks, prioritized international travel during vacations, and had always talked about an epic round-the-world backpacking trip, I was ready for us to quit our jobs, sell our house, and spend a couple years wandering the globe. My husband, on the other hand, absolutely loved that we were finally settling into a house we'd recently purchased, our careers, and a community after so many years in grad-school limbo.

While we didn't agree on what to do next, we did agree that we wanted each other to be happy and fulfilled in our careers and life together without either of us having to settle or give up what was most important to us.

At first, it seemed like one of us was going to have to give up our dream. If we moved abroad, my husband would "lose"; if we stayed at home, it would be me who'd miss out. Neither was acceptable, and I became determined to find a win-win solution.

I started by reflecting on why I was so eager to quit the international education job I'd worked so hard for; why I've always felt happier, more satisfied, and more *me* when living abroad; why my identity was so wrapped up in being a world traveler; and why I struggled to put down roots anywhere (even abroad). I asked myself question after question after question…

- Who am I if I'm not living abroad?
- What does *global* mean to me?
- What does *home* mean to me?
- How do I want global and home to show up in my life?
- Besides travel, what else makes me interesting?
- What is it about travel and living abroad that I love so much?
- What else gets me fired up?
- Is global a place or a mindset?
- How can I live a global life no matter where in the world I am?

At the same time, I was reading Pamela Slim's *Body of Work: Finding the Thread That Ties Your Story Together*. In the third chapter, Pam explains how to identify the ingredients that "add competence, distinction, emotional depth, strength, and meaning to the way we live each and every day." While Pam didn't explicitly address living a global life, I was intrigued by the "ingredients" idea. So I started brainstorming the ingredients I needed for a meaningful, satisfying, and sustainable global life.

I made a long list of everything I wanted in my life—all the feelings, experiences, people, connections, and personal and career goals I could think of. Then I reflected on what I'd most want in my life if I lived in the US, and what I'd want most want if I lived abroad. That's when I realized that I wanted the same things, no matter where I lived.

At first my list was fairly general and included things like travel, adventure, family, flexibility, and novelty. As I thought about what each of those things really meant to me, and how I wanted each one to show up in my life, I was able to be more specific. I then chose the top five things that I absolutely didn't want to live without, and they became my Global Life Ingredients. Here's the list I came up with at that time:

1. Aaron and I are equally happy and satisfied with our careers and life.
2. Spending quality time with my family in Oregon every year.
3. Being a part-time nomad, and traveling in the U.S. and abroad frequently for work and pleasure.
4. Building freedom and flexibility into my life and work (in order to accommodate 1-3).
5. Helping as many returnees as possible make re-entry a positive experience.

Once I identified my Global Life Ingredients, it was like a weight had been lifted off my shoulders! I felt more in control of my happiness because I no longer felt like I could *only* be truly happy abroad. I also threw away the outdated and limiting dichotomy of "home" vs. "abroad" (that's *so* last-century ;-)). Instead, I focused on creating a *life* I love no matter where in the world I happen to be.

When Aaron and I discussed our individual Global Life Ingredients, and why they were important to us, we started having deeper conversations and understanding each other better, which made it easier to work together to create a mutually satisfying life, in which neither of us has to settle or give up what's important.

I also realized that *global* is a mindset, not a place, and that simply being abroad doesn't make me global (just think about the people you've met who are abroad, yet live a very monocultural life). Sure, it's easier to live a global life when what you consider global is all around you 24/7. Yes, it takes creativity and determination to live a global life at home (but since when do world travelers back down from a challenge?). I found it freeing to realize that I have the tools and power to be global anywhere.

Our Global Life Ingredients became our compass and helped my husband and me make life decisions. Currently, Aaron and I are happily pursuing our careers in North Carolina because we decided that this is the best place for both of us professionally at this time. Aaron has the house, job, and community he craves (and which I now value and enjoy), while I'm able to spend quality time with my family in Oregon a few times year. We prioritize international vacations, and because my location-independent business supports my desire for freedom and flexibility, I'm able to spend anywhere from a couple weeks to a couple months working and traveling abroad each year. And, finally, I help returnees all over the world find their own Global Life Ingredients and make re-entry a positive experience every single day.

I no longer feel a tug-of-war between my need for wings and my husband's desire for roots because we figured out how to accommodate our most important ingredients for a meaningful global life. I also don't struggle with FOMO (fear of missing out) as much as I used to, because the things that are most important to me—the things that bring me the most satisfaction at this point—are part of my life.

While I look forward to living abroad again in the future, I love my current home and the global life I've created. I no longer feel like any roots that I put down will anchor me somewhere forever. And, because I now think in terms of living a global life, as opposed to being abroad (adventure!) vs. being at home (boring!), I don't struggle with re-entry like I used to. Rather than being a sad ending after spending time abroad, going "home" is now simply a mile marker on my lifelong global journey with ups and downs I know I can weather.

That's my story; yours will likely be different. Indeed, had I identified my Global Life Ingredients 15 years ago, my list would have included very different things (except freedom and flexibility—I've always been big on both of those). And I'm sure my ingredients will change in the coming years. That's the beauty of Global Life Ingredients; they represent what's most important to you right now and evolve along with you.

GLOBAL LIFE INGREDIENTS: FIVE REAL-LIFE EXAMPLES

I like to see examples when I'm doing something new; they inspire me, show me options I hadn't considered, and help me articulate things that I often feel but can't explain. I thought you might find it helpful to see other global adventurers' Global Life Ingredients. So here are five examples. (If you prefer to create without seeing examples first, skip ahead a couple pages.)

Michelle (BloggingAbroad.org) is a returned Peace Corps volunteer turned location-independent entrepreneur with her husband, Jedd. Here are her ingredients:

1. Prioritizing time, flexibility, and generosity over having money and stuff.
2. Lifelong learning, especially through interaction with different cultures and new experiences.
3. Staying in tune with global issues and using my U.S. citizenship to advocate for a more just world.
4. Going somewhere new at least once a year.
5. Exploring warmer climates during the winter and being "home" during Oregon's best season: summer.
6. Practicing a foreign language at least once a week.

Jedd (IntentionalTravelers.com) is a returned Peace Corps volunteer turned location-independent entrepreneur with his wife, Michelle. Here are his ingredients:

1. Flexibility of time to live the life I want to live: to spend time with loved ones; to take care of myself; to be able to do work that I enjoy and am passionate about; to explore.
2. Cooking as a way to learn about a new culture, practice and master a craft, and feed my other passion...eating.
3. Traveling and discovering somewhere new every year.
4. Becoming the best global citizen I can be through education: studying a new language, getting to know people from different countries and cultures.
5. Living with intentionality: Every day I make choices that are in line with the things that are most important to me.

Pouneh (LongingToTravel.com) is a PhD candidate at a university in the Netherlands and currently lives in Sweden with her husband. Here are her ingredients:

1. Adventure. I need that feeling you get when the plane is about to land or when you book a flight. Excitement. Adventure. Endless possibilities.
2. Professional fulfillment. My husband and I must feel a sense of purpose wherever we are.
3. Lifelong learning. It's critical to surround myself with new ideas, well-informed people, and learning opportunities.
4. Diversity. Of food, people, cultures, languages, religions, viewpoints—I need it!
5. Travel. Of course, I must always travel locally and internationally as long as possible.

Deidra (AtHomeInTheWorld.us) is a returned Peace Corps volunteer, transformative travel coach, and mother of two living in Vermont with her Costa Rican husband. Here are her ingredients:

1. Curiosity. I feel a sense of wonder about what is happening in the minds and hearts of those I love, my community, and the wider world. I love to talk with people and to learn about people, places, and ideas through reading and watching movies.
2. Connection. I engage regularly with people, places, and causes that are important to me. This includes traveling, volunteering, and meeting with people locally and virtually.
3. Contribution. I do work that helps people use travel and intercultural experience as catalysts for good in their own lives and in the lives of others.
4. Creation. I constantly look for ways to add beauty and creativity to my life, play with my kids, cook foods from around the world, make art, and write.
5. Introspection. I take time, often in nature, to understand what my experiences mean to me and what I want to do next.

Katie (YellowRubberBall.com) is a web developer, artist, and traveler living in Durham, North Carolina, with her husband and young daughters. Here are her ingredients:

1. New physical experiences—trying new foods, finding new outdoor adventures.
2. Connecting with people outside my culture—understanding new worldviews, [and experiencing] new music, art, and dance.
3. Feeling like I've gotten to experience a solid sampling of the cultures on our planet. I want to feel like I enjoyed as much as I could of the world.
4. Feeling connected enough with other world cultures to feel like an active participant of the world, an active world citizen—not just an American.
5. Physically getting on a plane and traveling.

Are you ready to find *your* Global Life Ingredients? Great! Let's dive in!

HOW TO FIND YOUR GLOBAL LIFE INGREDIENTS

Good news—you've already done more than half the work! The reflection activities you completed in the previous section laid the groundwork for pinpointing your unique Global Life Ingredients.

Next steps? First, you'll question your assumptions about *global* and *home*, then you'll reflect on the things (and people) that are most important to you at this point in your life.

Before we go on, I want to stress that, in order to identify your Global Life Ingredients and find your best next step, you must be willing to be very honest with yourself so you can get to the core of what you *truly* want your life to look like. This isn't always a quick and easy process. It's far simpler to get hung up on what we think our ideal global life should look like or model it after someone we admire. It's worth it in the end, though, to be true to yourself!

QUESTIONING ASSUMPTIONS

In this section, you'll question your assumptions about and expand your perceptions of what *global* and *home* mean to you. Why? Because it's extremely easy to unknowingly lock yourself into limiting ideas that won't serve you in the process of finding your Global Life Ingredients.

This is embarrassing to admit, but several years ago I realized that I was still trying to live an outdated version of my ideal global life—one that fit great when I was 17, but not so much in my mid-thirties!

It wasn't until I questioned my assumptions about what *global* and *home* represented for me that I realized the global life I was still trying to make fit had become a size too small. Until that point, I hadn't questioned my assumption that I could only live a global life abroad, and that being in my home country would only lead to boredom and unhappiness. (Wow, was I wrong!)

This activity will help you break down your own mental barriers (if there are any) that could hold you back from identifying your Global Life Ingredients and creating your Forward Launch.

But first, I'd like to share three short case studies with you. I first interviewed Jessica, Pouneh, and Dale for a re-entry series I hosted on the Small Planet Studio blog. I'm sharing their stories with you here because I love the way each of them deeply questioned their assumptions in re-entry, and then used the self-knowledge they gained to create a global life that's perfect for them.

After the case studies you'll find two reflection questions to complete.

CASE STUDY #1: SEEING POSSIBILITIES

Jessica Plaunt lived in Spain twice before becoming a mechanical designer in Minnesota. She loved living in Spain—the cultural excursions, the *rebajas* (sales), and the salsa dancing. Especially the salsa dancing.

Re-entry was surprisingly difficult for Jessica. "It sucked, to say the least," said Jessica. "I thought, certainly, to come back to a place I had known for years couldn't be that hard!"

Jessica navigated relationship issues, language issues, and why-are-the-roads-so-wide-here issues. In fact, she talked about being abroad so much that her friends and family banned her from talking about Spain.

Jessica thought the best part of her life was over. After asking herself some tough questions, getting clear on what she wanted her life to be like going forward, and being open to new experiences, she realized that her adventures were only just beginning.

"I thought about the things I liked about being in Spain, and found I could find similar things within a one-to-two–hour drive from where I live now. I also went on a really fabulous trip that showed me that there are maybe places I can visit that I might like better than Spain. That thought had never really occurred to me until I visited these other places!

"Only really after I could say…yes, I wanted to stay in the Midwest because I like grass (I have a nice yard for my dogs!), my car (freedom of movement that wasn't going to take half of my salary), and being around my family, was I able to make peace with the fact that I wasn't in Spain.

"I now prefer to visit new places instead of returning to Spain, unless it's to visit my friends there. [Earlier,] I wouldn't even have been able to imagine these other adventures I've had! Several of the places I've been since then I didn't know existed, or I wouldn't have expected myself to go there—like Aruba, Egypt, or Kauai, HI. Now I can't stop talking about Kauai! Aloooooha!"

Jessica is a fantastic example of someone who created a satisfying global life as a result of figuring out the things and people that are most important to her at this point in her life.

CASE STUDY #2: GLOBAL IS A MINDSET

For over a decade, Pouneh Eftekhari has been moving between the United States and Europe. She's lived in Denmark, France, Spain (twice), Turkey, various cities in the United States, and her current country of residence, Sweden.

When Pouneh returned to the U.S. in 2010, after four years studying and working in Denmark, she was surprised that it took a good five years before she found closure from that experience abroad.

One thing Pouneh learned is that re-entry is more about a specific experience ending than returning home. As she sees it, re-entry "is simply a transition. It's not the end of global adventures as we know them. It's not something to fear. It's just a thing that you can't avoid…and it's something you can leverage to ensure that what comes next is truly fulfilling."

Once Pouneh gave herself permission to feel however she happened to feel in re-entry, it became easier to find closure with her previous experience abroad and move forward with pinpointing her Global Life Ingredients and creating a meaningful, satisfying global life. She also discovered that adventure is all around. And, most importantly, that we often have to create that adventure for ourselves.

In her early twenties, Pouneh was all about budget travel, cheap hostels, partying, and increasing her country count. "As long as I left the airport, I added it to my list of 'places I've visited.'"

Now in her thirties, Pouneh finds that living a global life is more about cultivating a truly global mindset than being in a specific location. "It's not only about living abroad and traveling—although I'm grateful I'm still able to incorporate both into my life. It's also about incorporating new points of view, traditions, and experiences into my life...which can be done in every city and in every country," she explained. Pouneh's biggest aha moment? Realizing that if she wants to live a global life, she can do it anywhere—even when she's at home in the U.S.

What I love about Pouneh's story is that she questioned her assumptions about what global meant to her, which led to a richer global life both at home and abroad.

CASE STUDY #3: A JUMPING-OFF POINT

Although Dale Davidson lived in South Korea before moving "home" to the United States at age 11, he considers studying abroad in France and teaching English in Egypt his first two major experiences abroad.

Dale loved studying abroad—especially all the travel that came with it. At that point in time, Dale described traveling and being abroad as a "wonderful, stress-free opportunity that offered all sorts of experiences."

Dale's differing experiences abroad, and subsequent re-entries, sparked deep reflection. Studying in France led him to question, and then later move away from, his long-held goal of becoming a Navy SEAL. Then, because he wasn't exactly sure what he wanted to do instead of the Navy, Dale jumped at a post-college opportunity to teach in Egypt with his girlfriend, thinking he'd figure things out while abroad. As opposed to his study-abroad semester, Dale described living in Egypt as "real life," where he had to set up an apartment, go to work each morning, and navigate daily life. Living abroad taught him "what it was like to establish a real life in a dramatically different culture."

Upon returning home, still unsure about what he wanted to do next, Dale realized he'd made several assumptions about the impact of travel and living abroad. As he explained it, "The most important thing I realized was that going abroad didn't really solve any problems or answer any questions for me. Living in Cairo was a great experience overall, but it still didn't give me any clues as to what I should do next."

By questioning his assumptions about travel and living abroad, Dale realized that "abroad" isn't necessarily an automatic key to happiness. "You won't magically just know a lot more about yourself and what you're 'meant' to do, and it's very possible that you could be using travel as an excuse for not making progress in other areas of your life," he explained. "This is one of the dangers of having a great travel experience abroad. You train yourself to escape problems instead of dealing with them appropriately. When your boss yells at you, you'll think, 'Screw it, I'm going to Thailand!'"

After moving back to the U.S., Dale learned how to put travel and living abroad in the "correct mental context," so he could use his experiences abroad as a jumping-off point to make meaningful progress in other areas of his life. Since then, he has embarked on numerous career and other adventures, both in the U.S. and abroad, that make his life meaningful and satisfying. Dale has, for example, spent time in Portland, Oregon; worked with camels (long story); lived in a youth hostel for several months in Washington, DC, while looking for his current job; and started a website called The Ancient Wisdom Project, among many other things.

Dale's biggest tip for others in re-entry: "Be honest with yourself and think about what travel and being abroad did and didn't do for you. You might find that the solution to whatever's troubling you isn't a lack of travel, but a lack of something else."

QUESTIONING ASSUMPTIONS ABOUT LIVING A GLOBAL LIFE

Using the space below, answer these reflection questions.

- What does *living a global life* mean to me?
- How have I lived a global life so far?
- What are some positive and negative aspects of how I've lived a global life to this point?
- What are my fears and concerns when it comes to (not) living a global life?
- What are some new and different ways I could live a global life in the future?

QUESTIONING ASSUMPTIONS ABOUT HOME

Using the space below, answer these reflection questions.

- What does *home* mean to me?
- How have I incorporated home into my life so far?
- What are some positive and negative aspects of home?
- What are my fears and concerns when it comes to home?
- What are some new and different ways I could incorporate home into my life?

"Home isn't a place, it's a feeling."

~ Cecelia Ahern

HOW DO I WANT "HOME" TO SHOW UP IN MY LIFE?

HOW DO I WANT "GLOBAL" TO SHOW UP IN MY LIFE?

HOW CAN I ENSURE THAT I HAVE BOTH HOME ROOTS AND GLOBAL WINGS NO MATTER WHERE I LIVE?

WHAT (AND WHO) IS MOST IMPORTANT TO ME NOW?

When you return home from abroad, well-meaning people often ask what you're going to do next. Change careers? Go back to school? Buy a house? Have a child? Start a business? Get married? Retire? Settle down? Move abroad again?

While there's nothing inherently wrong with these questions, they do reinforce certain assumptions about the way we think about our lives. Instead of thinking in traditional life categories (e.g., career, family, travel, etc.), I suggest a different approach.

Consider, instead, the following four areas:

JOY	CONNECTION
What fuels me and makes me feel alive?	Which relationships do I want to nurture?
MASTERY	**LEGACY**
What do I know and what can I do as a result of living abroad?	What kind of impact do I want to have on the world?

Now it's time to reflect on what fuels you and makes you feel alive, what you know and can do as a result of being abroad, which relationships and connections are most important to you, and the impact you want to have on the world. Reflecting on these four questions will help you identify your Global Life Ingredients.

"Certain things catch your eye, but pursue only those that capture the heart."

~ Ancient Indian Proverb

JOY

Many returnees lament not feeling as "alive" at home as they did abroad and wonder if moving abroad again is the only way to feel the sense of adventure and engagement they crave. (That's the assumption I worked from for years.)

Here's the thing. Catching the next flight to Tokyo won't solve this problem. Simply going abroad again won't ensure that you'll feel alive, just as staying home doesn't mean you're destined to spend the rest of your days in a rut. The key is to identify what made you feel alive abroad and then integrate those things into your life going forward, no matter where you are.

In the space below, write down everything that fuels you, brings you joy, and makes you feel alive.

MASTERY

When you spend time abroad, you learn new things every single day. How to navigate an unfamiliar transit system, go grocery shopping when you can't understand food labels, get internet installed in your apartment. Sometimes it's easy to articulate what you've achieved, but most of the time you get so caught up in daily living that you don't realize just how much you've learned along the way. This is your opportunity to take a step back and take stock of your knowledge, skills, and abilities.

In the space below, write down everything you know and can do as a result of having lived abroad.

CONNECTION

We all need to feel connected. When considering the kind of global life you want to live, it's important to think about the relationships that are most meaningful to you, and how you can nurture them so they grow stronger, no matter where in the world you are. I'm not just talking about human relationships. Consider what makes you feel connected to something larger than yourself, such as nature, animals, faith, traditions, groups, work, adventure, ideas, causes, and so on.

In the space below, write down all of the connections that are important to you.

LEGACY

What kind of impact do you want to have on your friends and family, community, or the entire world? Maybe it's earning a lot of money so you can donate to worthy causes. Or perhaps it's spending more time with your partner and young children, helping aging parents, starting a business that serves a great need, or volunteering around the world. Maybe it's simply bringing joy to those you interact with each day. Whatever the activity, your legacy is something important to you that makes an impact on others.

In the space below, describe the kind of impact you want to have.

MY GLOBAL LIFE INGREDIENTS

You've reflected on your emotions, identity, and mindset. You've questioned your assumptions about *global* and *home*. And you've identified what fuels you and makes you feel alive, what you know and can do as a result of being abroad, the relationships and connections that are most important to you, and the impact you want to have on the world.

Now it's time to use all that information to identify your Global Life Ingredients!

The first step is to use the space below to list all the things that you *must* have in order to feel that you're living a meaningful, satisfying, and sustainable global life, no matter where in the world you are. Since everything you've reflected on in this workbook has laid the groundwork for identifying your Global Life Ingredients, you may want to flip through the workbook so you can review your reflection. You may also want to go back and look at the sample Global Life Ingredients.

The next step is to narrow down your previous list. Circle the three to five most important and meaningful items from your list above. Then, using the space below, drill down and describe each one in more detail. These prompts will get you started.

- How does this ingredient add meaning and satisfaction to my life?
- How would I feel if it weren't a part of my life?
- What are various ways this ingredient could show up in my life, no matter where I am?

Once you've identified your top three to five Global Life Ingredients, add them to your Re-entry Roadmap (which you'll find at the end of this workbook).

Still not exactly sure what your Global Life Ingredients are? Don't worry! You might just need a little more time to reflect. Take as much time as you need. Here are three tips to consider as you let your Global Life Ingredients percolate:

1. Identifying three to five ingredients is a general guideline. If you come up with more or fewer, that's totally ok.

2. You'll probably come up with fairly broad categories at first (e.g., adventure, speaking another language, travel, keeping in touch with friends, etc.). If that works for you and gives you enough direction, that's great! For most people, however, it helps to drill down further and make your ingredients as specific as possible. Remember, you can always update them as your life evolves.

   Here's an example. If travel is an important ingredient, ask yourself, "What kind of travel is important to me? Solo backpacking? Yearly luxury vacations? Visiting a new country every quarter with my partner and kids? Taking an extended travel sabbatical every five years?" Getting as specific as you can will make it easier to find your best next step.

3. The best question you can ask yourself is *why*. If you get stuck, ask yourself, "Ok, but why?" And then keep asking… "I really love travel." Ok, but why? "Because it makes me feel alive and happy." Ok, but why? "Because I'm really present when I travel." Ok, why? "Because travel engages all of my senses." Ok, but why? And so on…

Congratulations, you've identified your Global Life Ingredients.
Now you're ready to use them to create your Forward Launch!

Section 4: MY FORWARD LAUNCH

USING YOUR GLOBAL LIFE INGREDIENTS AS A COMPASS

Now that you have your Global Life Ingredients, let's talk about how to use them as a compass to find your best next step—what I call your Forward Launch. Before we get to that, though, I'd like to share Katie Benedetto Jones's story about how she used her Global Life Ingredients to create her ideal global life.

A NOMAD WITH A HOME

As told by Katie: I spent a good number of years thinking that I could either be a nomad or have solid roots. If there were any middle ground, I unthinkingly assumed I knew the recipe: That my husband would need to travel the world with me as a nomad himself; that we would afford travel by selling or renting our house. When he didn't want to do this—despite the [good] fortune that we both actually happen to have location-independent careers—it felt tragic. I felt like I was being asked to give up my dreams. I felt trapped.

It was all too easy to assume that I was stuck, when really, I was making too many assumptions. And as with many things in my life, when I started asking the right questions and opening up to new possibilities, the pieces fell into place.

When I worked with Cate, the author of this workbook, she introduced me to the concept of a global life. The idea instantly clicked with me—it was much more about getting really, really clear about what it is that I actually want—what it would take for me to feel like a global citizen—and satisfying that.

I love strategies that take this approach. Tim Ferriss influenced my idea of wealth by challenging whether I really want a sports car or the experience of driving down the 101 with my guy, wind blowing in my hair. Hands down, it's the experience that's far more gratifying. Danielle LaPorte does the same in the Desire Map, by asking how I want to feel—not what I want to accomplish. It's far more gratifying to go straight to the positive feeling than to assume that a particular action—for instance, creating a successful startup—is necessarily going to lead to that feeling.

The strategies that lead to greater awareness ultimately lead to more satisfaction for me. It turned out that creating my global life was similar.

I dug deeper into the nuts and bolts of what this global life personally means for me, and laid out a plan—one that feels solid, and big enough to provide a lifetime of expanding my global awareness—without requiring that I leave my roots.

For me personally, a large portion of my global life is about spending more time around non-European people, cultures, and events. So much of that is available right here in my hometown. A lot of my need for travel is based in a need for more international connectedness—and that's satisfied by some surprising local things, ranging from exploring the history of European dominance at an anti-racism workshop, to simply having a good conversation with the owner of an Indian market.

My global life includes learning new languages and exploring sociology in order to learn how to think differently. It includes serving internationally by expanding my work to international clients and giving to international charities. Finally, it includes planning trips as if I'm going to take them. So much of what I love about travel is the feeling of making the unknown known, of making somewhere completely new, that's scary in its unknownness, into a new, safe home away from home. Just planning a trip—I feel it as I plan my own upcoming trip—helps to make that connection, and connect with the humanity of a new place in the world.

Finally, a key component of my global life is actual travel. While I've learned that I really do prefer to keep to my home and my roots for most of the year, I still crave the physical adventure of planes, airports, and everything new! Traveling helps me set up little bits of home and roots around the globe. One big month-long trip per year seems, so far, to be about the right amount for me. A key component of making a yearly trip happen and making it work for everyone—for myself, my husband, my clients—was communication. With great communication, I found that I was pleasantly surprised at how well all the pieces fit and my goals worked out!

If there's one piece of wisdom I'd like to share about creating a global life, it's what I've learned from Cate: Creating a global life is not at all about settling; it's actively the opposite. It's about letting go of what I think I know about the solution to a problem, and digging deeper to get to a much better solution.

CREATING YOUR FORWARD LAUNCH

Your Global Life Ingredients are the three to five things that are most important to you and give your life the most meaning and satisfaction, no matter where in the world you are. This section will show you how to use these Global Life Ingredients as a compass for creating your Forward Launch.

I use my Global Life Ingredients as my compass all the time. I've moved towards some professional or travel opportunities because they supported my ingredients, and away from others because they didn't. When I feel FOMO (fear of missing out) creeping in and I'm frustrated that I'm not backpacking around the world *right now*, I review my ingredients and remember that I *am* doing what's *most* important to me right now. And when I'm pitching a trip abroad to my husband, he knows that one of my important ingredients is being a part-time nomad, and that traveling helps me appreciate the roots we're putting down (which is one of his ingredients). We make decisions together quickly and easily because our ingredients give us a starting point, a direction, and evaluation criteria.

To use your Global Life Ingredients as your compass, first you need to have an idea of what you'd like your next step to be. Use the space on the next page to brainstorm everything you could or would like to do next.

Some examples might be *find a job in a study abroad office, teach abroad, buy a condo, save money for a round-the-world trip, have kids, build up my retirement savings, retire early, spend time with my family, go to grad school, become a skilled home cook, buy a property to rent out while I travel, take a career sabbatical, run a marathon, volunteer, learn Arabic, get a dog,* etc.

This isn't the time to edit yourself! Write down **everything** that comes to you. Think expansively so you see all of your options.

I want to note here that while some people find this kind of activity a cinch and can dream up all sorts of next steps they could take, others find it more difficult. If that's you, don't despair! You're more of a practical dreamer. Try this: start with your current life and describe what you like and what you'd like to change. Then brainstorm potential next steps from there.

Now, from your brainstorm on the previous page, list the three to five potential next steps that you're most interested in pursuing.

1.

2.

3.

4.

5.

The final step is to evaluate your top potential next steps against your Global Life Ingredients. Use the following pages to reflect on the degree to which each potential next step offers the conditions that support your Global Life Ingredients. As you complete the worksheets on the following five pages—there's one for each potential next step—here are a few questions to consider:

1. **In what ways does this potential next step offer the conditions that support your Global Life Ingredients?** And does it support all five? Only one? A couple but only kinda, sorta?

2. **How could you modify this potential next step so it better aligns with your Global Life Ingredients?** For example, if one of your ingredients is nurturing your relationship with your niece and nephew while they're young, yet you really want to teach in Thailand, perhaps you could schedule a weekly Skype date and make visiting in person a few times a year top priority.

3. **If this potential next step doesn't align with your Global Life Ingredients, how ok are you with that?** Are you willing to sacrifice one or more of your Global Life Ingredients to take advantage of the opportunity? If so, for how long? In what case would you *not* be willing to make that sacrifice?

4. **How would you rate this next step numerically?** If 1 = least aligned with your Global Life Ingredients and 10 = most aligned with your Global Life Ingredients, what numeric value would you give the potential adventure?

The Re-entry Roadmap

POTENTIAL NEXT STEP #1

IN WHAT WAYS DOES THIS NEXT STEP OFFER THE CONDITIONS THAT SUPPORT MY GLOBAL LIFE INGREDIENTS?

IN WHAT WAYS DOES THIS NEXT STEP _NOT_ OFFER THE CONDITIONS THAT SUPPORT MY GLOBAL LIFE INGREDIENTS?

HOW COULD I MODIFY THIS NEXT STEP SO IT BETTER ALIGNS WITH MY GLOBAL LIFE INGREDIENTS?

HOW I RATE THIS NEXT STEP: 1 2 3 4 5 6 7 8 9 10

The Re-entry Roadmap

POTENTIAL NEXT STEP #2

IN WHAT WAYS DOES THIS NEXT STEP OFFER THE CONDITIONS THAT SUPPORT MY GLOBAL LIFE INGREDIENTS?

IN WHAT WAYS DOES THIS NEXT STEP *NOT* OFFER THE CONDITIONS THAT SUPPORT MY GLOBAL LIFE INGREDIENTS?

HOW COULD I MODIFY THIS NEXT STEP SO IT BETTER ALIGNS WITH MY GLOBAL LIFE INGREDIENTS?

HOW I RATE THIS NEXT STEP: 1   2   3   4   5   6   7   8   9   10

POTENTIAL NEXT STEP #3

IN WHAT WAYS DOES THIS NEXT STEP OFFER THE CONDITIONS THAT SUPPORT MY GLOBAL LIFE INGREDIENTS?	IN WHAT WAYS DOES THIS NEXT STEP _NOT_ OFFER THE CONDITIONS THAT SUPPORT MY GLOBAL LIFE INGREDIENTS?

HOW COULD I MODIFY THIS NEXT STEP SO IT BETTER ALIGNS WITH MY GLOBAL LIFE INGREDIENTS?

HOW I RATE THIS NEXT STEP: 1   2   3   4   5   6   7   8   9   10

The Re-entry Roadmap

POTENTIAL NEXT STEP #4

IN WHAT WAYS DOES THIS NEXT STEP OFFER THE CONDITIONS THAT SUPPORT MY GLOBAL LIFE INGREDIENTS?

IN WHAT WAYS DOES THIS NEXT STEP *NOT* OFFER THE CONDITIONS THAT SUPPORT MY GLOBAL LIFE INGREDIENTS?

HOW COULD I MODIFY THIS NEXT STEP SO IT BETTER ALIGNS WITH MY GLOBAL LIFE INGREDIENTS?

HOW I RATE THIS NEXT STEP: 1   2   3   4   5   6   7   8   9   10

The Re-entry Roadmap

POTENTIAL NEXT STEP #5

IN WHAT WAYS DOES THIS NEXT STEP OFFER THE CONDITIONS THAT SUPPORT MY GLOBAL LIFE INGREDIENTS?	IN WHAT WAYS DOES THIS NEXT STEP *NOT* OFFER THE CONDITIONS THAT SUPPORT MY GLOBAL LIFE INGREDIENTS?

HOW COULD I MODIFY THIS NEXT STEP
SO IT BETTER ALIGNS WITH MY GLOBAL LIFE INGREDIENTS?

HOW I RATE THIS NEXT STEP: 1 2 3 4 5 6 7 8 9 10

MY FORWARD LAUNCH IS...

After evaluating potential next steps, are you ready to declare your Forward Launch? If so, you're ready to finish your Re-entry Roadmap (see below)! If not, don't worry. Re-entry and creating your Forward Launch isn't always a quick, clear, or linear process. Keep reflecting and refining, practice some loving self-care, and reach out to me and the Small Planet Studio community if you'd like some support. Keep going—you *will* get there!

HOW TO FINISH THE RE-ENTRY ROADMAP

You've reflected on your emotions, identity, and mindset. You've identified your Global Life Ingredients and created your Forward Launch. It's now time to complete your personalized Re-entry Roadmap! You'll find the complete roadmap starting in the next section.

Once you've finished all seven pages, print or cut each one out of the workbook, tape them together, and you'll have your complete Re-entry Roadmap. If you feel inspired to do so, have some fun personalizing your roadmap using colored pens, pencils, watercolors, or other creative materials.

SEVEN TIPS

1. Review your Global Life Ingredients regularly to see if they still reflect what's most important to you. Update your ingredients as you grow and as your life evolves.

2. Use each re-entry—even if you're just returning from vacation—as an opportunity to review your Global Life Ingredients and make updates.

3. Create a list of Global Life Ingredients with your partner or family, in addition to your personal list.

4. Display your Re-entry Roadmap (or at least the last page) where you'll see it every day so your Forward Launch stays top-of-mind.

5. Keep your Global Life Ingredients front and center. Write them in your planner. List them on an index card that you keep in your wallet or purse. Hang them on your fridge!

6. When you feel restless or unsatisfied or when FOMO starts kicking in, refer back to your Global Life Ingredients and remind yourself that—for now—you've got (or are working towards having) the things that make your life truly meaningful and satisfying.

7. This workbook can help you through other life transitions, too. When you're facing another major change, go through the activities again, replacing *re-entry* with the new transition (e.g., *graduation, marriage, divorce, life with kids, empty nest, etc.*).

I have been impressed with the urgency of doing. Knowing is not enough; we must apply. Being willing is not enough; we must do.

~ Leonardo da Vinci

Section 5: MY RE-ENTRY ROADMAP

The Re-entry Roadmap

My Return
(How I feel. How I want to feel.)

What Fuels Me & Makes Me Feel Alive

What I Know & Can Do Now

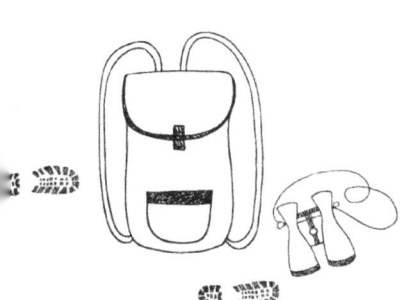

The Connections & Relationships that are Important to Me

The Re-entry Roadmap

The Impact I Want to Have on the World

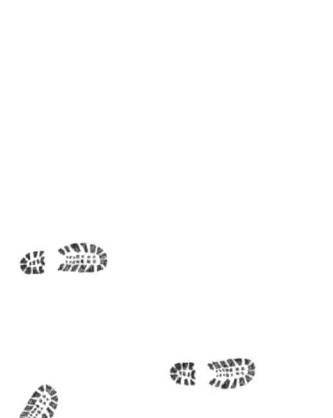

My Global Life Ingredients

My Best Next Step
(Forward Launch)

Section 6: NEXT STEPS

The Re-entry Roadmap

> *"It's your place in the world; it's your life. Go on and do all you can with it, and make it the life you want to live."*
>
> ~ Mae Jemison

CONGRATULATIONS!

You've completed the Re-entry Roadmap. Before we wrap up, let's check on what you'd hoped to accomplish when you began this workbook. Take a quick look at page 27. Did you get what you wanted to out of it?

____ Yes! I accomplished what I'd hoped when I started this workbook.

____ No, I didn't accomplish what I'd hoped when I started this workbook.

If yes…great!

If not…don't worry!

It could be that your goals changed as you completed the workbook. Or maybe the activities you initially skipped would now help you reach your goals. Or perhaps additional support is just what you need right now. If that's the case, here are a few options for finding more support and guidance on your re-entry journey:

1. **Download your bonus materials** at https://smallplanetstudio.com/rr-bonus

2. **Connect with fellow returnees!** Join our Facebook group, one of our small group programs or get one-on-one coaching. You'll find information about all three on the bonus page.

3. **Talk with a therapist** who understands the challenges of global living and international transitions. You'll find information about how to find a qualified therapist at the url above.

I wish you the very best!

Cate

ABOUT THE AUTHOR

Dr. Cate Brubaker is a re-entry (repatriation) coach and consultant, author of the Re-entry Roadmap creative workbook and the Study Abroad Re-entry Toolkit, co-author of Arriving Well: Stories about Identity, Belonging, and Rediscovering Home After Living Abroad, and CEO of Small Planet Studio, LLC.

She helps returnees turn the hardest part of the entire living abroad experience—*going home*—into a transformational one full of actionable insight and deep meaning. In addition to working with individual returnees, Cate leads workshops for groups of returnees and creates custom re-entry programs for organizations.

Cate has lived, studied, worked, and traveled in 37 countries on 4 continents. For over 20 years, she's helped all kinds of globetrotters, from students to teachers to corporate executives, successfully navigate international and intercultural transitions.

Cate's sweet tooth is as big as her global heart, which is why she also shares *recipes with a sprinkle of travel* on her other website https://www.InternationalDessertsBlog.com/ She's always thinking about where to travel next and never says no to a hot cup of tea with milk or a big scoop of gelato.

To contact Cate, email her at cate@smallplanetstudio.com. She'd love to hear from you!

Limitations live only in our minds. But if we use our Imaginations, our possibilities become Limitless.

Jamie Paolinetti

www.ingramcontent.com/pod-product-compliance
Lightning Source LLC
Chambersburg PA
CBHW062132160426
43191CB00013B/2274